IMAGES
of America

BILOXI

IMAGES
of America

BILOXI

Jamie Bounds Ellis and Jane B. Shambra

ARCADIA
PUBLISHING

Published by Arcadia Publishing
Charleston, South Carolina

Library of Congress Control Number: 2009921495

For all general information contact Arcadia Publishing at:
Telephone 843-853-2070
Fax 843-853-0044
E-mail sales@arcadiapublishing.com
For customer service and orders:
Toll-Free 1-888-313-2665

Visit us on the Internet at www.arcadiapublishing.com

Biloxi is dedicated to Adam, David, Danna, Daniel, my grandparents, Deirdre, Bill, Ed, Stephen, Chris and Lynn, Lilly, Alex, Chloe, Bailey, Dylan, Otto, and May.

CONTENTS

ACKNOWLEDGMENTS

Many individuals and organizations helped make this book possible. The authors would like to especially thank Charline Longino, head librarian of Biloxi Public Library, for her enthusiasm for this project and for her continued support. Also recognized are the Harrison County Library System director Robert Lipscomb and the board for their encouragement of the growth of the Local History and Genealogy Department. The collections of the department were developed under the care of retired local history and genealogy librarian Murella Powell, and without her attention to collecting historic photographs in the community, this project would not have been possible.

Several Biloxi historians donated their personal collections to the Biloxi Public Library so that the public could learn from their years of research. These historians and community leaders include Julia Cook Guice; Walter Fountain (1920–2003); Ruth Huls Hunt (1918–2007), former historian for the Biloxi Public Schools; and Zan Skelton. Many of the images in this book are included because of their commitment to preserving the history of Biloxi. The authors' appreciation goes as well to Biloxi Public Schools superintendent Dr. Paul Tisdale for his dedication to the continued development of the Biloxi Public Schools Collection at the Biloxi Public Library, as pictures from the collection were utilized in this book.

Thank you to the City of Biloxi, Mayor A. J. Holloway, and the Biloxi City Council for their interest in preserving Biloxi's history and your support for the local libraries. The authors appreciate the work of Vincent Creel as he connects the world to Biloxi's history through the City of Biloxi's Web site, a tool the authors used regularly for this book.

Katie Shayda, the authors' editor at Arcadia, guided them through the book writing process, and they wish to thank her for her patience and availability to answer any and all questions they had along the way. Thank you to Robert Adam Ellis for proofreading *Biloxi* prior to publication. Unless otherwise noted, all images in this book are courtesy the Biloxi Public Library.

INTRODUCTION

Biloxi is a walk through time and the streets and scenic past of Biloxi, Mississippi, an important part of the Mississippi Gulf Coast. Settled by Pierre LeMoyne d'Iberville in 1699, Biloxi has a rich cultural heritage that includes the first people of this area, the Native American tribe known as the Biloxi Indians. European settlers would not have been successful without the help of the Native Americans of this area. With cultural influences from Native Americans, France, Spain, and England during Colonial times, a unique culture emerged, one that is identifiable with other cities along the Gulf of Mexico including New Orleans, Louisiana; Mobile, Alabama; Pensacola, Florida; and Galveston, Texas.

Biloxi is located on a peninsula and across Biloxi's Back Bay in southeastern Harrison County; the county formed in 1841. In addition to Biloxi's Back Bay, other waterways include the Tchoutacabouffa River, the Biloxi River, and Big Lake. The Mississippi Sound serves as a buffer between Biloxi and the Gulf of Mexico and is rich with marine life. Biloxi's borders have expanded beyond the original city lines of the late 1890s with the additions of West Biloxi, Edgewater, North Biloxi, and the Woolmarket community.

Images of businesses, storefronts, and streetscapes document Biloxi from the late 19th century through the 20th and into the 21st. Downtown Biloxi is prominent in the following chapters, as it speaks to the history of the times. When downtowns thrived, Biloxi's Howard Avenue bustled with businesses and people. As suburbs became more popular and cities sprawled, downtown areas changed, and this was certainly true for Biloxi as well. Howard Avenue, known as Pass Christian Road in the 1890s, and particularly the section known today as Vieux Marche Mall, served as the major retail center prior to Edgewater Mall's construction in the 1960s and the expansion of the city west and north after World War II. Keesler Air Force Base, once on the edge of the city, was one of the reasons for Biloxi's expansion, and this also had a large impact on the area economically, culturally, and socially.

The streets of Biloxi have a history all their own. Street names have changed, and street numbers were changed in 1989 to comply with E-911 regulations, so identifying the placement of older structures can prove a trying experience at times. This became even more evident after the destruction of Hurricane Katrina, when many individuals strove to understand the history of their homes. Whenever possible, the authors strive to include information in the image captions as to whether the address is old or new.

Beach Boulevard, repaved and restriped with new curbs and sidewalks during 2008 and 2009, has been identified by different names over the last century. This scenic boulevard is also known more formally as Highway 90. Several sections of this boulevard have been named in honor of hometown heroes and innovators. Sections are dedicated to Apollo 13 astronaut Fred Haise and civil rights leader Dr. Gilbert Mason Sr. (1928–2006), both pioneers of the 1960s.

Interstate 10 also runs through Biloxi, and the Interstate 110 loop's southern end begins in Biloxi and ends in the city of D'Iberville. The I-110 bridge replaced the former Back Bay bridges of 1901 and 1927 that linked Biloxi to the farming country. The I-110 loop memorializes J. A.

"Tony" Creel and Sen. John C. Stennis. Connecting to the northern end of I-110 is Highway 15, designated as the Wade Guice Memorial Highway in 1997 in memory of the former Harrison County civil defense director.

Another notable figure from this area is potter George E. Ohr. Ohr worked and lived in present-day downtown Biloxi, and his pottery now has an international following. He lived on Delauney Street in the early 1900s, and a section of the street has been renamed George E. Ohr Street. The Frank Gehry–designed Ohr-O'Keefe Museum of Art is just around the corner on the Biloxi beachfront.

Hurricanes are a natural part of being situated on the Gulf of Mexico, and Biloxi has seen quite a few. Photographs from the hurricane of 1947 and 1969's Hurricane Camille show that the coast has been devastated by natural disasters before Hurricane Katrina. Images from Hurricane Katrina are also included to give a visual survey of downtown Biloxi in October 2007.

Some properties documented in this book no longer exist; however, the growth and rebirth of Biloxi is evident with the survival of places and monuments everywhere. The Biloxi Lighthouse, built in 1848, survived and still shines bright, but the Dantzler House, built in 1849 and located just to the northeast, did not survive Hurricane Katrina.

Tourism has always played an integral role in Biloxi's economy. Wealthy visitors from New Orleans first came by boat to the Mississippi Gulf Coast for vacation and second homes in antebellum Biloxi. Grand hotels were built along the beachfront in the 1910s and 1920s. In the 1950s and 1960s, the emergence of nightclubs and tourist court motels changed the tourist landscape once again. Gaming was part of the culture all along, although it was hidden before gambling was legalized in the 1990s. Now casinos line areas where seafood factories once stood in east Biloxi. Tourists from all over visit this area for a variety of reasons, and casinos, beaches, condos, golfing, fishing, hotels, and restaurants are all available for visitors and citizens alike.

Parades are an important cultural aspect of this entire area, and Biloxi has long celebrated Mardi Gras. Many Biloxians enjoy Mardi Gras balls, and parades are a festival open to all who would like to just have fun. Many of the parade images in this book exhibit the backdrop of downtown Biloxi businesses. Other parades in Biloxi history included the Firemen's Day parades and holiday parades, such as Christmas and St. Patrick's Day.

Constantly changing and adapting, Biloxi will continue to thrive in the future. Faced with either tough or booming times, Biloxi always assimilated to new eras. Although this book focuses on the special times of Biloxi's past, there is much more to celebrate and experience in the years ahead.

One

BILOXI BUSINESSES
AND PLACES

Many of the images in this chapter show the lively streets of Biloxi in the early 1900s, but the pictures span from the late 1800s through 2009. Included among the pictures are businesses, local people, churches, schools, and government buildings. Each image holds a key to the long history of Biloxi and speaks to the diversity and endurance of its people.

Of particular focus are the businesses of downtown Biloxi in the early 20th century. From a survey of these places and streets, the changing face of downtown is evident. Also included are individuals and organizations that have impacted and influenced the cultural growth of the city.

The U.S. Post Office, Courthouse, and Customhouse, built between 1904 and 1908 on land purchased from William Armstrong in 1902, served as Biloxi's federal building through the 1950s. Construction was delayed by the hurricane of 1906 and a yellow fever epidemic. In these images, the ground is cleared and workers prepare for the construction of the marble, stone, and iron structure. It was officially dedicated in August 1908. Biloxi postmaster J. C. Tyler was charged with the care of the building in March 1908; he served the federal government in several different capacities during his career, including special prohibition agent and U.S. Marshal. He was also influential in establishing rural routes for mail delivery in the outlying areas around Biloxi, which are actually within the city limits today.

The phases of construction are seen in these images as the columns of the classical revival–style federal building are completed. On April 2, 1960, the structure was officially dedicated as Biloxi City Hall, and it still serves this function today at 140 Lameuse Street. In 1978, the building was listed on the National Register of Historic Places, and in 2008, Biloxi mayor A. J. Holloway and the City of Biloxi celebrated the structure's 100th anniversary. The City of Biloxi is currently engaged in a plan to renovate and restore the building to ensure that it is enjoyed by many generations to come.

Depicted here is the intersection of Reynoir Street and Howard Avenue in downtown Biloxi around 1907. In the center of the postcard is a westbound streetcar, which was operated by the Biloxi Electric Railway and Power Company of Lameuse Street. A sign for George W. Klare's Real Estate Agency (the second building from the left) is visible at the southeast corner of the intersection.

Lines of cars parked next to downtown businesses fill the sides of Howard Avenue in this 1938 picture. The grand architecture of the First National Bank of Biloxi is seen on the right, and its sign states that it is the "Oldest Bank on the Mississippi Coast." Today the building has been renovated and restored to its original look, and it is presently BancorpSouth.

Businesses flourish in this *c. 1952* photograph taken at the corner of Lameuse Street and Howard Avenue. The Rexal Drugs sign on the right advertises the Kimbrough and Quint Drug Company. The next business to the left is the American Restaurant, and the Hawaiian Lounge is situated to the left of the restaurant. In the center of the photograph, the First Bank of Biloxi sits high above the surrounding buildings.

A glimpse of 1940s Biloxi is available by looking east from the intersection of Reynoir Street and Howard Avenue. The Lopez Building (right) hosted many businesses throughout the time period, including insurance and physicians' offices. Grant's Drugs (left), owned by William J. Grant, proved to be a long-lasting business on Howard Avenue. Grant also served as the secretary of the Oyster Commission.

Ford Model Ts are parked on a city street between the trolley tracks and the sidewalks in the 1920s. The second car from the left is the coupe version of the Model T. Approximately five chickens enjoy their freedom on the empty lot, and a vendor works nearby (right). Houses surround the area with features such as chimneys, clapboard siding, and functional shutters.

Road repair work takes place at the intersection of Reynoir Street and Howard Avenue in this c. 1925 photograph. The streetcar tracks are prominently shown in the center of the image, and the bricks are piled in neat stacks on the sides of the street. The workers appear to be predominantly African American, and they worked intensely to complete the project.

Joseph Morice's grocery store, then located at 133 East Howard Avenue, is the subject of this *c.* 1923 image. The building stood at the corner of Howard Avenue and Main Street. Under the sign that reads "Joe Morice Cash Grocery" (center), a chalkboard is visible. Near the back of the building (right), a sign reads "Shoe Repairer." Biloxi City Hall (right) is recognizable because of its distinct canopies.

Looking south on Howard Avenue between Porter and Benachi Avenues is the back of the scenic Maloney-Dantzler property. The Maloney-Dantzler House, originally built in 1849, was located on Beach Boulevard near the Biloxi Lighthouse but is not visible in this picture. On the expansive grounds in the 1910s or 1920s, a visitor would find livestock, gardens, and a gazebo (right).

Located on the north side of city hall on Main Street around 1920, this shop (center) was owned by J. M. Jalanivich, tinsmith. A 1919 advertisement in the *Daily Herald* stated that he was also a sheet metal worker and that his copper work was "properly done." He also specialized in automobile repair and roofing projects.

At the northwest corner of Reynoir Street and Howard Avenue, T. P. Dulion Mercantile Company operated an expansive clothing and goods store. The mercantile company offered millinery, an elevator to navigate the three-story building, and an "exclusive" cloakroom. Sales peppered the advertisements in the local newspaper consistently, and the company's wares included everything from contemporary fashions to home furnishings.

November 17, 1890, was the opening night of the Masonic Opera House by the Magnolia Lodge No. 120 A.F.&A.M. Three stories high, the front of the building boasted glass windows, arched doors, and a seating capacity of 575. Also contained within the building were meeting rooms on the third floor for the local Masonic lodge and business offices.

On August 20, 1892, a musical soiree was held for the benefit of the Cathedral of the Nativity of the Blessed Virgin Mary at the Opera House. Admission was 50¢. The image shows the set of the musical comedy *The Stragglers*, performed by H. H., R. J., and J. A. Maloney, James Conner, and W. Herbert. Also on the program for the benefit were piano, violin, and vocal numbers by performers from the Golden, Maloney, Thurber, and Cooper families.

George Edgar Ohr (1857–1918), known as the "Mad Potter of Biloxi," was hailed as the pottery wizard in his 1918 obituary in the *Daily Herald*. He won a silver medal at the St. Louis Exposition in 1904 for his unique pottery. The image above shows his art pottery studio at 400 Delauney Street (now Rue Magnolia). His funeral service was held at the Church of the Redeemer, and he was buried in the Biloxi Cemetery in a simple grave.

Owned and operated by N. P. Henley, the Biloxi Bakery, also known as the Original Spanish Bakery, specialized in bread, cakes, hard tack, fancy pastries, and pies. Depicted here is the bakery's wagon in 1895. Located at the corner of Pass Christian and Main Streets, the bakery offered customers a delivery service at no extra charge. Henley also served as the city clerk of Biloxi in the early 1890s.

Men with their horses and buggies fill Main Street in this 1895 photograph. S. Bradford operated a stable and served as a blacksmith, gunsmith, and practical horse shoer. Carriage painting was another specialty service offered by Bradford. Notice that many of these services are painted on the shutters of the business (left). The livery stable and undertaking business was located on Main Street near Pass Christian Road, which is presently Howard Avenue.

The Biloxi Automobile Company (left) was located on Lameuse Street north of Jackson Street, and a few of the automobiles for sale were displayed on the street. Under the same roof was shoemaker Antonio Bertucci's shoe repair business (center). Just to the south of these two businesses were the Biloxi Plumbing Company and Smyly and Myer Real Estate (right).

This Howard Avenue store must have specialized in cigarette sales, as Piedmont Cigarette signs are plastered on the side and front of the building. Also on the side of the structure is another tobacco-related advertisement that says, "Roll 'Em Yourself." Notice also the Coca-Cola signs in the area that show bottles for sale for 5¢.

The streetlights are turned on for the first time in the Edgewater Park subdivision in the late 1920s. Originally, Edgewater was its own community between Gulfport and Biloxi, but it is now within the Biloxi city limits. The Edgewater Gulf Hotel, built in 1926, was located to the west of the subdivision.

West End School, an early Biloxi school, was located on Porter Avenue near Cemetery Street, and it was donated by Lazaro and Julia Lopez in 1898. The school was first intended for children younger than the third grade who lived west of Cuevas Street. Sidewalks were built in front of the school in 1917.

Built between 1912 and 1913, Biloxi's Central High School was dedicated on November 14, 1913, in the school's auditorium. Among the speakers were state superintendent of education J. N. Powers, Biloxi's city superintendent of education R. P. Linfield, and philanthropist Harry T. Howard. This image is from 1938, when the principal was A. E. Scruggs, and the superintendent of the Biloxi Public Schools was George W. Ditto.

Ada Moore's first-grade class at Gorenflo Elementary School poses for a class picture on October 25, 1937. The classmates are, from left to right, (first row) Walter Quave, Mary Anglado, Ethel Chinn, Ida Mae Gandy, Barbara Hamilton, Edward Thibodaux, Vera Toncrey, Mary Adamo, and W. A. Boudreaux; (second row) Iona McQueen, Earl Forehand, Doris Ladnier, Robert Nielson, Eugene Brewer, Lionel Jermyn, Emile Wiltz, Jerry Foster, Eunice Herbert, Leverne Stephens, and Gerald Fryou.

Children at Gorenflo Elementary School in the 1950s eat lunch in the school cafeteria. It appears that the children's well-rounded lunch consisted of a sandwich, a piece of cake, and an apple. Some of the children were most likely students of teacher Ada Moore. Gorenflo was originally constructed in 1924, and a new elementary school named Gorenflo replaced the building in 2003.

Located on Beach Boulevard and Bellman Street, the Episcopal Church of the Redeemer was first organized in 1851. Charles and Harry T. Howard donated the church property and buildings, and the family of Jefferson and Varina Davis donated a silver communion service to the church. The church was heavily damaged during Hurricane Camille. A Hurricane Camille memorial on the front lawn of the church was dedicated just days before Hurricane Katrina on August 17, 2005. The beautiful church grounds include the Ring in the Oak tree at the front of the property, which is bestowed with a legend about love and acceptance between the Biloxi and Pascagoula Indians.

The children and adults pictured here are from the Sunday school at the black First Baptist Church, then located at 403 East Railroad Avenue, around 1931. According to the writing on the chalkboard in the center of the image, Rev. H. P. Williams served as the pastor and W. H. Hannibal was the church clerk and superintendent of the Sunday school at the time the picture was made.

The Presbyterian Church of Biloxi officially formed on May 17, 1891. The building pictured here on East Howard Avenue was constructed after the congregation formed. The congregation met at the old Methodist church building in the interim. The new church at 1340 Beach Boulevard was dedicated in 1962.

The grounds of the First Baptist Church of Biloxi are prepared for the construction of the new church building at 917 West Howard Avenue. Groundbreaking ceremonies were held on February 4, 1924. The Bond-Grant House (right), once part of the church property, was moved across Howard Avenue; it has been renovated and is now owned by the City of Biloxi. The church is located on Popp's Ferry Road in north Biloxi.

The Chau Van Duc Buddhist Temple (right) is located at 179 Oak Street, and it sponsors the Mid-Autumn Moon Festival in Biloxi. Adjacent to the temple is the Vietnamese Martyrs Parish (left), founded in 2000. Both churches serve the Vietnamese community of Biloxi. After the end of the Vietnam War in 1975, many Vietnamese immigrants moved to this area, and they continue to be an integral part of the community.

New Municipal Library,
Biloxi, Miss.—19

On June 1, 1925, the Biloxi Library moved from the Creole Cottage to its new building at 124 Lameuse Street. The building was designed by the prolific Biloxi architect Carl Matthes. At the formal opening, Mayor John J. Kennedy, librarian Bridges, and New Orleans city librarian Henry M. Gill were present. City librarians who followed Bridges included Virgie Fayard in 1926 and Florence Freidhoff in 1931.

Beginning in 1898, Biloxi boasted the first free public library in the state of Mississippi. It was free in the sense that patrons did not pay subscriptions to use materials in the library. The Creole Cottage (center) came into service in 1900, after the first building was destroyed by fire, and was operated by the King's Daughters Biloxi Circle. The Biloxi Library was located in the rear building from 1977 through 2005.

Two

BEACH BOULEVARD AND THE MISSISSIPPI SOUND

Beach Boulevard is the scenic byway that connects Highway 90 travelers to the natural beauty of the Mississippi Gulf Coast. The Mississippi Sound has long been a source of nourishment, with its plentiful seafood and amusement along its man-made beaches for visitors and locals alike. Protected by the barrier islands, the boulevard, beaches, and sound combine together in relaxing harmony.

Enjoy a trip along the historic beachfront with the selection of images in this chapter. In this chapter and in others, many images are labeled West or East Beach; Lameuse Street served as the dividing line for all east/west streets in Biloxi prior to 1990. Also notice the many forms of transportation in these pictures; readers will find schooners, trolley cars, and automobiles navigating the coastline in this series of images.

The trolley operator carefully maneuvers his electric car on its tracks as it turns west along Beach Road. In 1911, adult riders could pay the Gulfport and Mississippi Traction Company a mere 50¢ for a ride from Back Bay and Point Cadet to Pass Christian. The total trip lasted three hours. Tickets could be bought in advance from local merchants. The Biloxi Herald Band furnished music for the occasion.

This electric trolley provided a breezy mode of transportation for both tourists and locals connecting to trains in adjourning cities. By 1910, the *Daily Herald* reported that trolley cars were running between Pass Christian and Biloxi. For an hour-and-a-half trip, the cost of a one-way ticket was 40¢, and a round-trip ticket was 75¢. Riders with luggage were charged an additional 5¢.

Long, wooden piers have been and still are prevalent along the beaches of Biloxi. Even for those shy of the water, these high piers provide viewers a bird's-eye view of aquatic life below. Prior to the days of sunscreen, beachgoers were compelled to bring straw hats with wide brims to shield their skin from the intense reflected sunshine.

Tourists and residents have always been attracted to Biloxi's beaches. Beachwear fashion has certainly changed through the decades, but the water has always offered occasions for relaxation. Also to be recognized are the shallow waters adjoining Biloxi's shores, affording fun activities for all age groups.

Taken at Beach Boulevard and St. Paul Street, this image dates to the 1910s. An automobile is parked on the dirt street between the beachfront homes. The home at left nearest to the vehicle was renovated after Hurricane Katrina, and it stands as a fine example of the historic homes of the beachfront. The Presbyterian Church of Biloxi eventually relocated to the property next to the house (left).

On display here is West Beach Biloxi just one block south of Father Ryan Avenue, and this area is located to the west of White Avenue in Biloxi. Seashore Methodist Campgrounds were located to the west of these homes. Looking east, notice the trolley tracks and power polls near the beach.

Named after the White family, who were the original owners of the buildings and first operators of the hotel, the White House Hotel was built on West Beach between White and Morrison Avenues. The 1914 Sanborn Fire Insurance Company map indicates that the complex was equipped with steam heat and electric lighting and that a night watchman provided hourly rounds for safety. In 1936, room rates ran from $4 to $7 per day.

This modern Biloxi Yacht Club structure, completed in 1901, was located on the beach across from the Montross Hotel. During this year, a magnificent three-day regatta was held that included boat races of all kinds. Music, dancing, and food were all a special part of the celebrations. Soon after its opening, a great hurricane visited Biloxi. Fortunately, the new structure stood sound, and only the wharves were damaged.

In 1927, the Tivoli Hotel was built on East Beach. Surrounded by an array of majestic oak trees, its southern view was that of Deer Island. The 1927 city directory listed the "absolutely fire-proof" hotel as having 120 outside rooms and 24 apartments combined to offer multitudes of amenities including a barbershop, a children's play room, a tennis court, croquet, riding facilities, and accessibility to golf courses.

Before the advent of the seawall, one could sit comfortably near the water's edge and enjoy the sights and sounds of the nearby waterway. Narrow streets worked well for minimal traffic counts. Swaying moss suggests a gentle southern breeze. High piers were available for fishing, walking, and careful diving. Far in the background is Deer Island.

The *I. Heidenheim* sails across the Mississippi Sound among oyster luggers at right. Below, it sails south from the Biloxi Yacht Club. The schooner participated in the sailing races and regattas of the 1920s on the Mississippi Sound. It was scheduled to participate in the July 15, 1928, Gulf Schooner Championship, a 50-mile race that began at the Biloxi Yacht Club; it was entered into competition by the Peoples Bank and the Mississippi Power Company. Isadore Heidenheim, the namesake of the schooner, was a prominent Jewish businessman in Biloxi in the early 1900s. He served as an alderman for the City of Biloxi in the 1910s and also managed the Sea Food Packaging Company. Heidenheim died in Biloxi in 1918 at the age of 61 and was buried in his native city of New Orleans.

A ship sails the Mississippi Sound between Deer Island and the coast of Biloxi. Where canning factories once stood, casinos now inhabit the same area. The smoke stacks from the various canning factories are visible on the right, and it becomes evident that the companies operated in close proximity to their neighbors.

The schooners docked in this picture are the *James J. Lemon* (left) and the *Myrtle Lowis* (right). Schooners were often named for local leaders and family members and could be named after males or females. Dr. James J. Lemon, originally from England, operated a drugstore in downtown Biloxi. Emile Davies mastered the *Myrtle Lowis* according to a 1913 registration in the Customs Office.

From the shoreline of the Biloxi beach, a view of Deer Island is available. The island has weathered many storms and has survived them all. Hurricane Elena and Hurricane Katrina caused particular damage and erosion to the island. After Katrina, many of the island trees turned brown as a result of the saltwater intrusion.

The schooner *Perfection* sails ahead during a race on the Mississippi Sound. A July 22, 1918, article in the *Daily Herald* noted that *Perfection* was a new schooner built and owned by Henry Brasher. In that particular race, it finished with a time of 6 hours, 19 minutes, and 17 seconds. The winner, the *H. E. Gumbel*, had a time of 6 hours, 6 minutes, and 59 seconds.

very hard fun getting fat from
such good treatment. Lillie.

The Seashore Methodist Campgrounds, a popular destination for revivals, is shown in this 1906 postcard. The postmark, dated October 19, 1906, notes that Natchez was the destination of this particular card. Both the First United Methodist Church of Biloxi and the Seashore Methodist Assembly met on the grounds at different times.

Here is another view of a Biloxi Yacht Club regatta and schooner race. In addition to the sailing races, motor races were also run in the 1920s. In 1928, the festivities took place on July 10 through 11 and July 15. Great crowds gathered near the Biloxi Yacht Club to view the exciting races.

Three

HURRICANES

Hurricanes, like other natural disasters elsewhere, have always been and will always be a part of living along the Gulf of Mexico's coastline. Although the next storm to impact the area cannot be predicted, one thing is certain: Biloxians will continue to exhibit resiliency and recover from whatever comes their way.

The images in this chapter include the hurricane of 1947, Hurricane Betsy (1965), Hurricane Camille (1969), and Hurricane Katrina (2005). The hurricane of 1947 is unnamed, as Atlantic hurricanes were not named at that time. Hurricanes were exclusively named after women until 1978, when male and female names were rotated.

The hurricane of 1947 made landfall on September 19, 1947, and left a path of destruction across Mississippi and Louisiana. In this image, debris litters Beach Boulevard to the east of Porter Avenue. The Biloxi Lighthouse (left), the Biloxi Chamber of Commerce (center), and the Maloney-Dantzler House (right) all suffered damage from the storm.

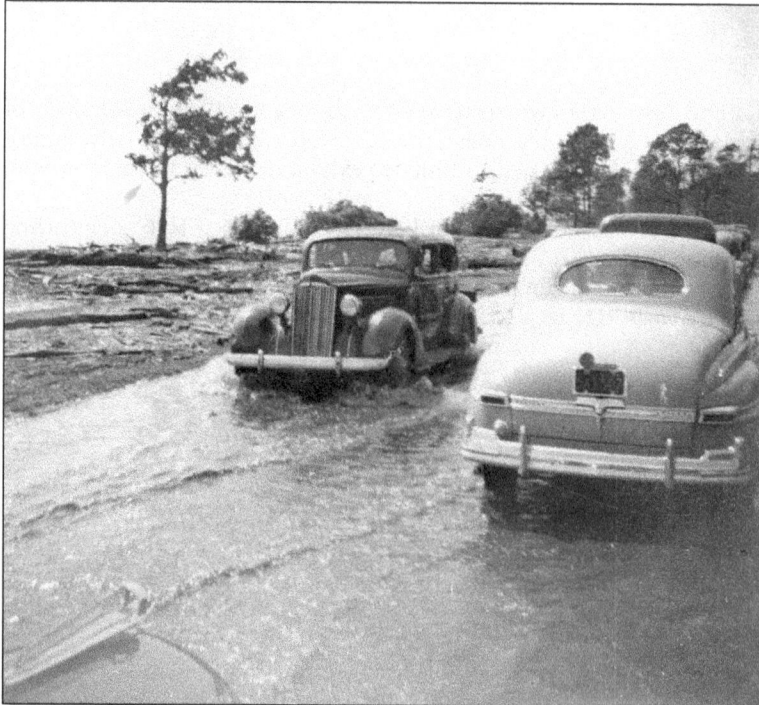

Automobile drivers try their best to navigate the flooded streets in the aftermath of the hurricane of 1947. Debris from buildings and fallen trees along Beach Boulevard found a final resting place upon the sand of the Biloxi Beach. When hurricane waters retreat, the beaches are always filled with unusual artifacts from the storm.

Atop the Buena Vista Hotel, which received damage to its beachfront rooms and facade, a view of the impact of the hurricane of 1947 on downtown Biloxi can be seen. Beach Boulevard is a watery mess, with automobiles and wood scattered about. John Gimma Plymouth (left), the Bungalow Restaurant (center), and Baricev's Restaurant (right) all received major damage from the storm.

The New Marietta Café (left) is missing doors and windows from the hurricane of 1947. A Budweiser Beer sign leans toward the building. In the foreground, pipes from a washed-away building remain. Citizens and soldiers survey the ruins of houses and businesses in the area. Managed by Agnes Barnes in 1940, the café was located at 631 West Beach Boulevard.

A boat landed near the front lawn of the Biloxi Hotel after the waters receded from the hurricane of 1947. Boats and ships that can be relocated are often moved to Back Bay, but many are left on the beachfront because of lack of time to prepare and logistical concerns. During every storm, several boats become unmoored and wash ashore.

In September 1947, the remains of the 1901 wooden Back Bay Bridge are shown with the destruction they incurred. Waves reached a maximum height of 14 feet on the beach in Biloxi. H. D. Shaw, the engineer and architect of the seawall, reported the heights of waves in the *Daily Herald* article "Water Heights Measured in Hurricane Area" on September 29, 1947.

By September 27, 1947, over 6,000 airmen and officers from Keesler Field were helping the city of Biloxi cleanup after the 1947 storm. Here men survey the damage to Greyhound Lines bus no. 740 (center) under a collapsed roof. Notice the gasoline drum (left) that floated above ground. Many dangerous situations lurk after any hurricane or tropical storm.

The Gallott-Canaan Sea Food Factory (right) is flooded after an inundation of rain and winds from the hurricane of 1947. A sign painted on a building (left) notes, "No Children Allowed on Wharf." With the rising water and disturbed marine creatures, this spot was not safe for anyone on this September day in 1947.

Hurricane Betsy made landfall on September 10, 1965, in Grand Isle, Louisiana, as a category 4 storm with winds of 125 miles per hour. Flooding in the city of New Orleans was a major disruption to normal life. It still is the 35th most intense hurricane on record according to NOAA's National Hurricane Center. The storm caused damage on the beachfront in Biloxi, and this image shows the destruction of structures between Baricev's Restaurant, left, and the Buena Vista Motel, pictured on the right. Below is an example of the damage to downtown Biloxi streets post Hurricane Betsy. A sign (at left) shows that this street connects with Highway 15 and Highway 67.

Men gather outside of the Dukate School building after Hurricane Camille in 1969. Biloxi benefited with the help from the men at Keesler Air Force Base during the cleanup process, just as after the hurricane of 1947. Luckily for Biloxi, Keesler Air Force Base has the capacity and logistical resources to handle such disasters.

Hurricane Camille ransacked the Buena Vista Motel on the south side of Beach Boulevard. Camille made landfall in Hancock County, Mississippi, in the dark of night on August 17, 1969. It remains the second most intense storm in North American hurricane history, and the category 5 storm is number 15 on the list of deadliest hurricanes. Winds were estimated to have reached over 200 miles an hour.

Damage to the Biloxi–Ocean Springs Bridge was massive, and this image is looking southwest near the Biloxi side of the bridge toward the old Coast Guard hangar on Biloxi's Point Cadet (center). The terrible storm moved whole sections of the bridge, but the bridge was eventually repaired. Until Hurricane Katrina destroyed the bridge in 2005, motorists experienced a very bumpy ride as a result of the damage and repair.

Beauvoir, last home of Jefferson Davis, had debris strewn across its property, and the front gates are visibly smashed in this picture taken from Beach Boulevard, which is also known as Highway 90. The airmen who took these images of Camille were sent out into the community from Keesler Air Force Base by Julia Guice, former civil defense director. Her husband, Wade Guice, was Harrison County civil defense director during Camille.

A bowling alley on the eastern end of Biloxi's peninsula is washed out after Camille swept through the Gulf Coast. Depending on what caused the damage, the destruction could be very different to structures in the same area. Once onshore, hurricanes spawn many small tornadoes. This particular structure was ravaged by both wind and water.

As with other hurricanes of the modern era, the federal government supplied troops to help assist in the cleanup and management of post-storm activities after the landfall of Hurricane Camille. A soldier walks west on Highway 90 near the Gulf View Towers (right). A sign in the median of the road ironically reads "All Slow Moving Traffic Keep Right;" as one can see, there was not much traffic moving.

Cars move slowly behind trucks dedicated to recovery from Hurricane Camille. The westbound traffic is merging to avoid the debris near the Sun-N-Sand Motel (right) on West Beach Boulevard near Camelia Street. A sign for Trinity Baptist Church, located on Southern Avenue, is also visible (right). The Beth Israel congregation was also located just to the north of this picture at 401 Camelia Street.

St. Michael's Catholic Church, established in 1907 at Point Cadet, is shown after Hurricane Camille. Many of the shrubs on the lawn have turned brown from the invasion of saltwater on Point Cadet. In 2009, it is in the process of renovations from the damage received during Hurricane Katrina.

This photograph was taken in October 2005 in the wake of Hurricane Katrina from the top of the Biloxi Library's observation tower. Looking southwest, the Beau Rivage Casino is seen standing tall (top center). The back of Mary Mahoney's restaurant is seen surrounding the large oak tree (bottom center). Hurricane Katrina raged ashore on August 29, 2005, and it is recorded as the third deadliest hurricane according to NOAA's National Hurricane Center.

Looking directly south from the observation tower, the highly anticipated Hard Rock Casino and Hotel of Biloxi project is visible. The casino was within days of opening to the public when Hurricane Katrina struck, and it had to be rebuilt. It held its official opening on July 7, 2007, and the band 3 Doors Down kicked off the festivities on the opening weekend.

49

The view in this post-Katrina image is of Biloxi west of Lameuse Street. Biloxi Regional Hospital (right), located at the corner of Jackson and Reynoir Streets, was an extremely busy place in the midst of Katrina's damage. Debris, which took a great deal of time to cleanup, was still evident in October 2005; however, this was just a fraction of the trash that remained after landfall in August.

Crews actively worked in the Vieux Marche Mall (center) and on top of a section of the Biloxi Regional Hospital (left). In the distance, the Imperial Palace Casino (far right) is visible; FEMA staff used part of it as their conference area in the first months after the storm. Katrina was a category 3 storm when it made landfall, but the storm surge was well beyond expectations.

Four

MILITARY INFLUENCE

The Mississippi Gulf Coast's long affiliation with the military and the federal government is clear when a list of federal installations in the area are compiled. Biloxi's Keesler Air Force Base, originally Keesler Field; the Veterans Administration hospital; and the National Cemetery are long-lasting examples of this connection.

The Biloxi Lighthouse, just west of downtown, and Coast Guard Air Station Biloxi on Point Cadet are reminders of federal influence from a bygone era. The Biloxi Lighthouse, built in 1848, was operated by the U.S. Coast Guard from 1939 until 1968. Without the military, the coast would certainly suffer economically and socially, as it is an integral part of this area.

Construction was well underway at Keesler Field in 1941. Keesler Air Force Base was originally named Keesler Field on August 25, 1941. Keesler became an Air Force base on January 13, 1948. In 2008 and 2009, Keesler Air Force Base razed the former off-base housing and quickly replaced the housing by constructing modern homes in the various military housing areas in Biloxi.

Keesler Air Force Base barracks are in the foreground. Many airmen, officers, and civilians have lived or worked at Keesler Air Force Base since its inception. It was the setting for Neil Simon's play *Biloxi Blues*. Keesler, however, has constantly changed and adapted to new missions over the years since its initial creation.

The distinctive checker pattern on the water tower (right) indicates that this is an early image of Keesler Field, as Keesler Air Force Base was first known. The first group of men attending basic training at Keesler Field made their appearance on August 21, 1941, but the first officers arrived in June 1941. The 81st Training Wing calls Keesler home, as do the 403rd Wing's 53rd Weather Reconnaissance Squadron Hurricane Hunters and the 815th Airlift Squadron Flying Jennies.

Jeeps and trucks from Keesler Air Force Base assist in the cleanup efforts after the hurricane of 1947. They are parked at one of the seafood factories near Point Cadet. Supplies, equipment, food, and manpower were offered through the resources of the military base. In one instance in September 1947, sixteen thousand cupcakes were made available for cleanup crews.

A Schreck/Viking 00-1 Flying Boat is oriented to the southeast of U.S. Coast Guard Air Station Biloxi and points toward the hangar. Biloxi became an active air station on December 5, 1934. Only one plane remained after the site was downgraded to a detachment in 1947, and the base was decommissioned in 1966.

Anthony Ragusin snapped an aerial shot of U.S. Coast Guard Air Station Biloxi in the early 1940s. Behind the hangar, homes and canning factories dot the Back Bay landscape. Trees and homes blanket the area, but it was devastated by Hurricane Katrina, and many of the structures and trees are now gone.

A mechanic works one of the engines of what is likely the PJ-2 CG-51 *Antares* inside the hangar at U.S. Coast Guard Air Station Biloxi. The hangar was fireproof and was made of steel and concrete. The air station also assisted in rescues at sea and in military operations against U-boats in the Gulf of Mexico during World War II.

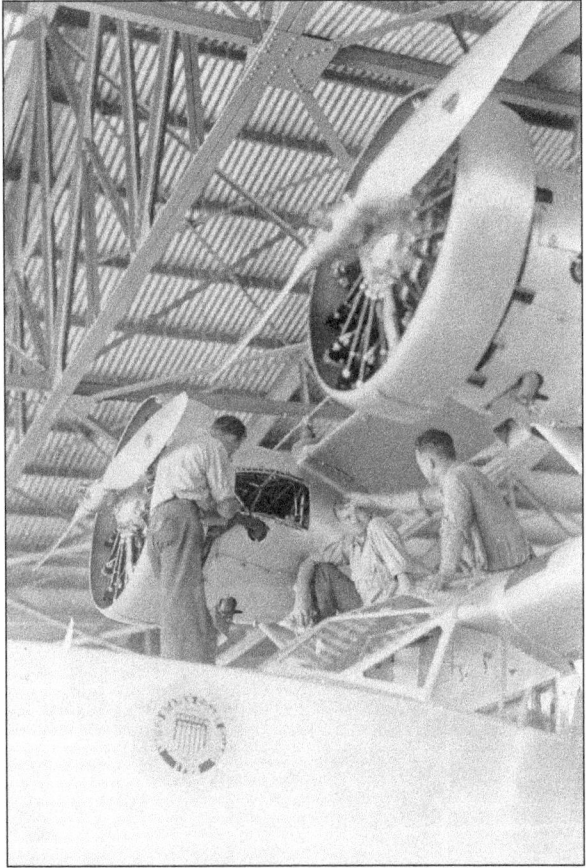

The Coast Guard's PJ-2 CG-51 *Antares* points toward the southeast on the airstrip of U.S. Coast Guard Air Station Biloxi in the late 1930s. The site continued to be extremely useful to the City of Biloxi, and in later years, the area was renamed the Point Cadet Plaza, and the Seafood Industry Museum was established in what had served as the barracks.

One of the buildings used as the Biloxi USO was located on the southeast corner of the intersection of Main Street and Beach Boulevard. A quick burning fire destroyed the building on August 19, 1966. The Biloxi Harbor is located behind this image, and prior to Katrina, McElroy's Restaurant served breakfast, lunch, and dinner in its harbor beginning in the 1970s.

The Veterans Administration established a hospital facility overlooking Back Bay in 1932 that is now known as the Veterans Administration Gulf Coast Veterans Health Care System. In 1934, the facility had a capacity of 567 beds, and in 2009, it serves 50,000 veterans. A beautiful site filled with native trees, the Biloxi National Cemetery is also located here.

Five

HISTORIC HOMES
AND STRUCTURES

Historic homes and structures can be found nestled throughout Biloxi, but they are most evident along the beachfront and in downtown Biloxi. There are many homes and places within the city that are listed on the National Park Service's National Register of Historic Places.

Hotels, churches, and bridges are just a few of the topics covered in this chapter. Tourism has long been a part of Biloxi and the Mississippi Gulf Coast, and the area has seen many different versions of tourist abodes. From watering places to grand hotels to the tourist courts and now to casinos, Biloxi has been an example of the changing trends in tourism.

The Biloxi Lighthouse, built in 1848, is a long-standing structure that has stood the test of time. Near Porter Avenue, the lighthouse is one of the most iconic structures in the state of Mississippi, and it shares a history with other lighthouses along the Gulf of Mexico. It was deeded to the City of Biloxi in 1968 and was added to the National Register of Historic Places in 1973.

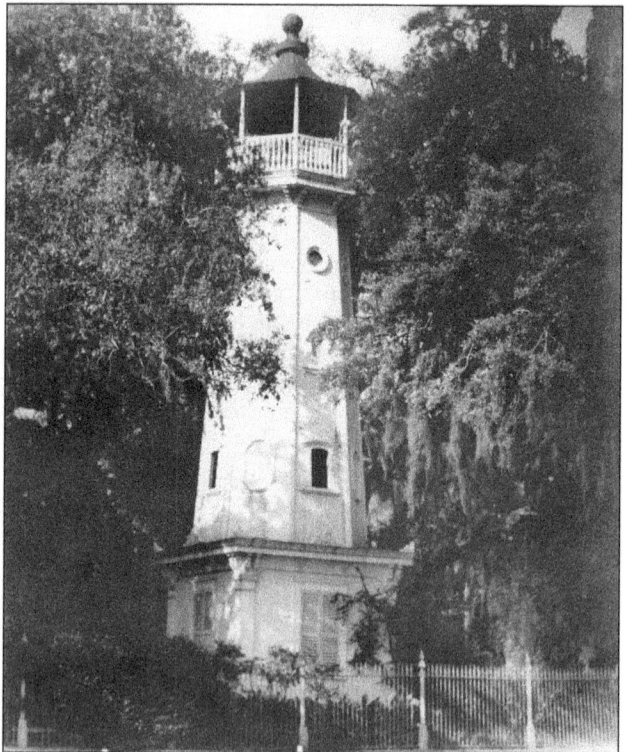

This photograph shows the famous Wood Lighthouse as it appeared on East Beach Road in Biloxi. It is appropriately named after its owner, A. Baldwin Wood, who purchased this property in 1912. Wood was known worldwide as the famous inventor of the Wood Screw Pump, designed to withstand the ravages of severe street flooding. This famous beachfront structure was substantially damaged in Hurricane Camille.

The Magnolia Hotel (at right), built around 1849, was originally located near the beach. Hurricane Camille swept out the first floor of the structure and caused massive damage in 1969; however, the structure was saved and moved to its present location facing Rue Magnolia, which used to be Magnolia Street. The building is shown below on Rue Magnolia in the 1980s. Through the 2000s, the first floor of the building was used as a Mardi Gras museum, and the upper floors were used for the City of Biloxi's historical administration department and the headquarters of the Gulf Coast Carnival Association. The structure was again damaged by Hurricane Katrina, but it fared much better than other structures of its kind in its protected location; it is one of the oldest surviving antebellum hotels on the Gulf Coast.

The Riviera Hotel, located at 101 East Beach Boulevard, was another antebellum hotel. It was formerly known as the Montross Hotel, and according to a 1904 Biloxi business directory, its style was the American plan, much like the nearby Magnolia Hotel. Judging and modeling for the ELKPAT Bathing Revues were held at the Riviera Hotel in the 1920s.

Known as the White Houses, these properties eventually became the White House Hotel. The White family, for whom White Avenue is named, owned and operated lodging for tourists. Located at 1550 West Beach Boulevard, the hotel once thrived; it was managed by Walter and John White in the 1930s. Golf, tennis, riding, fishing, bathing, boating, and dancing were amenities advertised for the hotel during that time.

An interior view of the Buena Vista Hotel is presented here. Arches abounded everywhere in the hotel, and large doors and windows graced the exterior. WLOX, Biloxi's ABC affiliate, first began broadcasting in a studio in the Buena Vista Hotel in 1962, but the hotel was destroyed in Hurricane Camille and the station moved to a new location.

The restored Victory Room, shown in this image, was used for many functions and dinners. The Buena Vista's facilities could comfortably accommodate conferences and special events. During the 1930s, the hotel advertised guest conveniences inside the hotel such as a convention hall, dance pavilion, arcade, beauty parlor, gift shop, and drugstore.

Opening on the Fourth of July weekend in 1924, the Buena Vista was a grand hotel with tan stucco decorated in a Spanish style. It was located at 800 West Beach Boulevard and was one of the few hotels with a telephone in the 1927 City Directory. Consequently, its telephone number was 1200. The hotel was situated on property just north of Beach Boulevard and was adjacent

to the I-110 bridge before it caught fire in the early 1990s and was subsequently torn down. The Beau Rivage Casino is now located just to the south of this area. During the 1960s, the Buena Vista Motel was built directly south of the hotel.

Located on Howard Avenue between Reynoir and Lameuse Streets, the Avelez Hotel was built around 1925. The site of the hotel was unique because it was situated among the central district of downtown Biloxi businesses. The hotel also was located on one of the busiest parade routes in the city, and would have been keenly positioned for carnival festivities.

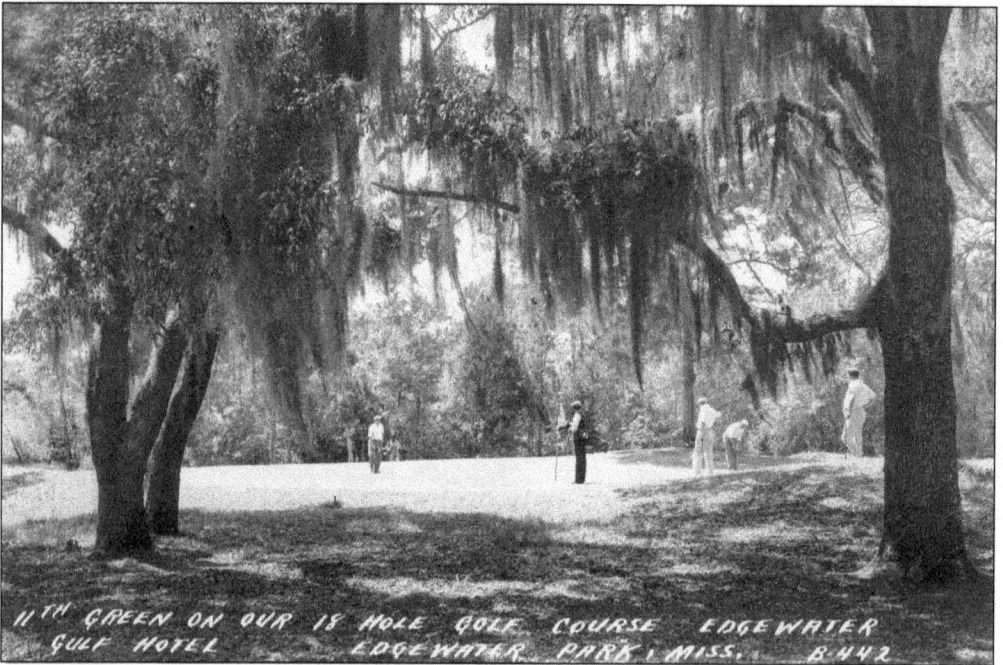

11TH GREEN ON OUR 18 HOLE GOLF COURSE EDGEWATER
GULF HOTEL   EDGEWATER PARK, MISS.   B-442

The Edgewater Gulf Hotel, built in 1926, was the sister hotel to the Edgewater Beach Hotel of Chicago, Illinois. Golfers in this image enjoyed the 11th green on the 18-hole golf course. The hotel was demolished in 1971, but not without resistance, as it did not fall on the first attempt. The golf course no longer exists, and the Edgewater Mall is now located on the grounds.

The Tivoli Hotel, opened in 1927 on East Beach Boulevard, was touted as a "unique family resort hotel with a club atmosphere" in the 1934 *Daily Herald* golden jubilee publication. The hotel rooms came complete with a kitchenette and private bath, and they could comfortably accommodate two to four people.

The Hotel Biloxi was originally operated as Dr. H. M. Folkes's Biloxi Sanatorium. Many hotels in the 1800s on the Mississippi Gulf Coast were known as watering places and specialized in spa treatments, taking advantage of the naturally occurring springs in the area. This structure is still standing, and it was converted into condominiums.

The Broadwater Beach Hotel was built in 1939 by Joe W. and Dorothy Brown of New Orleans and included a marina and golf course. Until Hurricane Katrina, the golf course was still operated by the President Casino. The Joe W. and Dorothy Dorsett Brown Foundation, founded in 1959, aids the homeless and the helpless and supports educational interests and community groups in New Orleans and the Mississippi Gulf Coast.

The Broadwater Marina was located south of the retro neon sign south of Beach Boulevard and the Broadwater Beach Hotel. Pres. Ronald Reagan stayed at the Broadwater Hotel in October 1984 while visiting the coast for a campaign rally before the presidential election that year.

The Marina Restaurant was located in the Broadwater Hotel's harbor through the late 1980s. The President Casino purchased the property and used the building for different purposes. The President Casino barge was located just to the south of the restaurant building at the opening of the harbor.

Beauvoir, the last home of the president of the Confederacy, Jefferson Davis (1808–1889), is located at the intersection of Beauvoir Road and Beach Boulevard in West Biloxi. Davis wrote the *Rise and Fall of the Confederate Government* on the grounds. It stands as the only National Historic Landmark on the Mississippi Gulf Coast. A museum and library are available for tourists to visit, and reenactments are held each year.

Navy captain John Walker (1834–1907) sits at right on the porch steps of his Seal Avenue home with members of his family. He was a prominent Biloxian, having served as mayor and as president of the Bank of Biloxi. He kept journals of the local weather and Biloxi events from 1857 to 1907, and they are at the Biloxi Public Library.

The Ring in the Oak tree is located in front of what was once the parsonage and continues to be the grounds of the Episcopal Church of the Redeemer. The Secretary Oak, another notable Biloxi oak tree, is located near DeMiller Hall on the rear of the property. In 1905, the pastor and church rector was Rev. J. S. Moore.

Biloxi's Central High School, seen between the 1890s and 1910s, was located on the southwest corner of Main Street and East Railroad Avenue. In 1905, it was one of six city schools, which included Back Bay School, the black school, the primary school also located on Main Street, Point Cadet School at Maple Street and East Howard Avenue, and the West End School on Porter Avenue.

Tullis-Toledano Manor, located on East Beach Boulevard, was a beautiful structure, and it was built between 1854 and 1856. Christobal Toledano and Matilde Pradat Toledano were the first occupants of the house. Later the Philbrick and Tullis families lived in the house. The City of Biloxi purchased the property in the 1970s, but the buildings were lost in Hurricane Katrina.

The Biloxi Lodge of Elks No. 606 was located on the southwest corner of Lameuse and Jackson Streets. The structure was demolished in the 1970s, and the 1977 Biloxi Library was built on the same site. The site is currently empty, as the library building was torn down in early 2009.

BILOXI COMMUNITY HOUSE,
BILOXI, MISS.—72

The Biloxi Community House, which also served for a time as the USO, was located to the east of Main Street on Beach Boulevard in downtown Biloxi. Many different structures in Biloxi served as the USO from the 1940s through the 1960s. The Maloney Dantzler House also hosted the USO at one time.

The Biloxi Hospital was located near Bellman Street on East Beach Boulevard and was dedicated on July 3, 1929. The Main Street Biloxi organization's 2008 Christmas ornament depicted the hospital at this location. Like the Episcopal Church of the Redeemer, a neighboring property, Harry T. Howard donated the land for the hospital. Before Hurricane Katrina, the facility was operated as the Biloxi Specialty Hospital.

Under the care of the Biloxi Council of Garden Clubs, the Old Brick House was rejuvenated in the 1950s and served as the Biloxi Garden Center. The property faces Biloxi's Back Bay, and it is located on Bayview Avenue. The house was added to the National Register of Historic Places in 1973, and it is presently owned by the City of Biloxi.

Volunteer Fire Company No. 1 of Biloxi formed on September 19, 1883, and this was their Lameuse Street firehouse. The building is identified as the Peoples Theatre, which opened on April 3, 1920. In August 1920, the film *Girl of the Sea* played at the theater.

The Spanish House, located at 782 Water Street, was most likely built in the 1840s, and is formally know as the Scherer House. The two-story brick house features stepped gables. On February 14, 2009, it was dedicated as Gallery 782 Co-Art, a program sponsored by Main Street Biloxi.

Mary Mahoney's Café (left), which was open 24 hours, is shown in this pre–Hurricane Katrina photograph. To the north is an adjoining courtyard between this structure and Mary Mahoney's Restaurant and a massive oak tree; the formal dining restaurant was one of the first downtown restaurants to reopen after Katrina.

The firehouse and fire engine for Mississippi Hook and Ladder Company No. 1 is shown in this picture. A junior fireman drives a small replica in front of the fire engine. The fire company was organized on February 21, 1890, with Biloxians from the Bellande, DeLamare, Redon, Henley, Lemon, and Dalton families, to just name a few.

The 1927 opening of the Back Bay Biloxi bridge is a festive occasion for the motorists and Biloxians pictured in the realm of excitement. Ford Model Ts lined up to be among the first to cross the bridge. This bridge replaced the 1901 wooden Back Bay Bridge. The 1927 bridge was made of

concrete and had streetlights. The official name of the bridge was the Biloxi-D'Iberville Bridge to differentiate it from the former bridge.

The opening of the 4,200-foot-long Biloxi–Ocean Springs Bridge in 1931 is the topic of this photograph. The two-lane concrete bridge was a great help to motorists. It was replaced by a new Biloxi–Ocean Springs Bridge that was dedicated at 4:30 p.m. on May 9, 1962.

Benachi Avenue—between Howard Avenue and Beach Boulevard and one street east of Porter Avenue—is a tree-lined historic Biloxi street. Zio Benachi of New Orleans owned the land that the street now occupies, and he vacationed in Biloxi from the 1890s until his death in 1923 at the age of 57.

The new Biloxi–Ocean Springs Bridge was built after the previous bridge was destroyed in Hurricane Katrina. The Mississippi Department of Transportation's two-year design/build project opened to traffic on November 1, 2007. The new bridge is six lanes and has pedestrian and bike lanes that are heavily used year-round. Biloxi is seen in the distance behind the bridge, as this image was taken from Ocean Springs.

The Biloxi Cemetery, located between Porter and White Avenues, was established near the beach, but is now on the north side of Highway 90. On some of the highest ground on the Biloxi Peninsula, the cemetery has benefited from more protection from storms. Students of Biloxi High School and community families perform cemetery tours and reenactments in May and October.

The Saenger Theatre, a performing arts center, is now a city-owned structure. It continues to provide an auditorium for performances and concerts by local and international groups. The Gulf Coast Symphony Orchestra, the Biloxi City Ballet, St. Patrick's High School, Biloxi High School, local dramatic groups, and the Community Concert series all utilize the restored facility.

Looking west, a row of seafood canning factories near Point Cadet Biloxi is the view in this photograph. This image gives a great overview of the proximity of the factories, and it illustrates the great number that once existed on Biloxi's front beach but are now practically extinct in that area except for a very few along Back Bay.

Six

PARADES
AND CELEBRATIONS

Along the Mississippi Gulf Coast, people are always looking forward to the next celebration. In this area, there are many activities and parades to attend. The Shrimp Bowl, the Blessing of the Fleet, St. Patrick's Day, and the Seafood Festival are a few of the festivities held annually in various city locales.

Mardi Gras parades in Biloxi are popular events that locals and visitors attend in great numbers every year. People on Mardi Gras floats throw everything from beads to snacks to those reaching up from the street along the parade routes. In addition to parades, lavish balls are thrown, and the year's royal courts are presented.

Biloxi Carnival 1928

On February 21, 1928, Mardi Gras had a grand noontime celebration in Biloxi. Mark Miller, the King d'Iberville, and Mercedes Wilkes, the Queen Ixolib (Biloxi spelled backwards), headed the royal court. Thousands of people welcomed this parade. A motorcycle squad, bands, mounted police, and floats also accompanied the king's float. This picture shows the stop at which the king was toasted at city hall and was presented the keys to the city.

Blanche Picard reigned as Biloxi's first Queen Ixolib for Mardi Gras in 1908. As a child, she lived on Main Street in the heart of Biloxi and graduated from Biloxi High School. She was the daughter of Sarah Picard. The same year as this photograph, Blanche married Sollie Edward Levy, a salesman and later an army captain, at the Presbyterian Church of Biloxi with a Hebrew ceremony by Rabbi Moses Bergman.

The 1929 Mardi Gras parade marches westward on Howard Avenue on February 12. The line of floats is followed by a stream of cars. The Kress store was located on the north side of the street. Spectators watch as the intricately decorated floats pass along the parade route in downtown Biloxi.

This 1927 photograph depicts the six maids who participated in the Gulf Coast Carnival Association's royal court. Elegantly dressed in the finest fashion from head to toe are, from left to right, Eulalie Castanera, Amelia Castanera, Eugenia Eley, Mercedes Wilkes, Elizabeth Tucker, and Cornelia Bolton Miller. Col. J. W. Apperson was King d'Iberville, Mildred Eley was Queen Ixolib, and Walter "Skeet" Hunt was captain this year.

In the 1960s, Howard Avenue was still a popular shopping place as well as a parade route. With the increase of vehicles, traffic signals were more abundant. Barq's Root Beer was a prominent icon along the path, and the Hotel Avelez can be viewed towering over the downtown businesses.

Keesler airmen march in parade formation along brick-lined West Howard Avenue during 1944. The onlooking crowd consists of both military and civilians. Looking from Magnolia Street toward the east, one can readily identify the Red Cross banners as well as a shoe store, an optometrist, a hardware store, and popular beer logos. The highway sign would not be found on this street today, since Highway 90 is now Beach Boulevard.

In this 1940s parade, police motorcyclists lead the way on a chilly day. The parade scene is located to the west of Reynoir Street and Howard Avenue. Biloxi Auto Parts (left) is one of the businesses in the image. A sign for the Saenger Theatre hangs about the decorated street.

Night parades were also popular during the Mardi Gras celebration in Biloxi. This float decorated in foil is shown rolling south on Main Street. The theme "Biloxi Warriors" appropriately reflects the historic Native American tribe that the explorer d'Iberville met when he approached the shores of Mississippi. Biloxi schools have appropriately utilized the Native American theme in their mascot selections. Riders on this float hail from the Slavonian Benevolent Association.

A photographer ambitiously took this picture from atop the Biloxi Lighthouse. Looking along Highway 90 toward the west, a long line of popular vehicles can be seen both in and along the parade route.

In 1962, the Gulf Coast Carnival Association parade had nine bands. Floats were decorated with papier-mâché and foil and were illuminated with electric lighting. At a royal banquet in the Hurricane Room of the Buena Vista Hotel, the following guests are seated, from left to right: Bartlo Hunt, Mr. and Mrs. Emile Fallo, Rev. Victor Augsburger, Mary Jane Augsburger, Mayor Daniel Guice, Margaret B. Guice, Walter Fountain, Matt Lyons, Anthony Ragusin, and Kenner Hunt.

Another celebration in which great food was laid out for a dinner is documented by this 1950s photograph. Potato salad, ham, and boiled shrimp are all perfectly prepared and ready to eat. Walter Fountain (left) and Walter Hunt (right) frame the picture. Conch shells decorate the table, and plates are stacked and waiting for the buffet line to start.

As part of Biloxi's annual Shrimp Festival, a reception and shrimp buffet is held at the Slavonian Benevolent Association of St. Nicoli for the judges, officials, and distinguished guests. A variety of shrimp dishes are prepared. In 1957, seventeen shrimp dishes were served, including jellied shrimp salad, Biloxi shrimp goulash, and green peppers stuffed with Biloxi shrimp.

The thirteen 1926 All Southern ELKPAT Bathing Revue contestants pose near the Riviera Hotel. Mabel Riley of New Orleans won first place in the competition, and she went on to compete in Atlantic City as Miss Biloxi. Upon winning, Riley received a large box of candies on behalf of the management of the Riviera Hotel and an engraved cedar chest.

One of the largest bathing revues of the ELKPAT Frolics was the 1928 pageant. Mildred Garrison of New Orleans was declared the winner, and Cherry Blossom of vaudeville fame won second place. During judging, the women walked a U-shaped platform and then walked down a small flight of stairs. The majority of entrants hailed from New Orleans.

In 1955, Mardi Gras fell on February 22. In celebration, a fireman begins to open a scrumptious mound of oysters with an oyster knife. This popular knife was an essential tool designed to efficiently open and remove the delectable treat. From left to right are Walter Fountain, Kenner Hunt, Matthew Lyons, an unidentified fireman, Walter "Skeet" Hunt, Anthony Ragusin, and an unidentified fireman.

In June 1918, several thousand people attended the celebrated launching of the *Elizabeth Ruth*, named after the daughter of Lord Lever of England. This 1,500-ton vessel was constructed by the Mississippi Shipbuilding Corporation on Back Bay. Catherine Lopez christened the boat with the traditional bottle of champagne. The Herald Band provided music, and guests were served light refreshments.

This picture from April 9, 1946, shows members celebrating the 38th anniversary of the Order of the Eastern Star Ann Grayson Chapter, which was established on April 9, 1908. The order is the largest fraternal organization in the world open to both women and men. The charter members at the table were, from left to right, Esther Rohrer, Justine Swetman, Claude Meaut, Stella Harkness, Electa Hass, and Kate Suter.

Coach John Williams (center) receives the trophy for the 1962 victory at the state football championship on behalf of the Biloxi High School team. Mayor Daniel Guice (left, first row) smiles as the students and football players celebrate. That same year, the football team also won the 23rd Annual Knights of Columbus Shrimp Bowl and was the South Division Big Eight Champions.

Walter Fountain prepares fireworks to celebrate a 1950s Shrimp Bowl. During the Shrimp Bowl, local football teams compete for the Shrimp Bowl title, and a Shrimp Bowl Queen is crowned. The celebration was always held at Yankee Stadium on Lee Street in Biloxi. In later years, the property held the Division Street Children's Library and City of Biloxi baseball and soccer fields.

A firemen's day parade marches through Biloxi past homes and businesses in the early 1900s. In this image, a streetcar is seen at right progressing along the parade route with the parade officials, horses, and citizens. The trolley tracks were located to the side of the main road. On the far right, Biloxians walk down the sidewalks and enjoy the parade.

The East End Fire Company's wagon was destined to be a parade float in an early Firemen's Day Parade in Biloxi. A sign on the fence at right shows that the scene is on Howard Avenue. The wagon's banner reads "Purity, Peace, Happiness." A young girl sits atop the wagon waiting for the parade to start.

The parade float for Volunteer Fire Company No. 1 is stopped in this c. 1915 photograph. The steam engine is decorated in flowers and streamers. A Sherwin Williams sign is located on the store next to the scene. Volunteer Fire Company No. 1 was on Lameuse Street.

In this view of the East End Fire Company's wagon with the little girl at the top, the float has moved. The house behind the parade has a sign that notes that it is for rent. A woman watches the activities from a second-story window. Biloxi adolescents stand near the back wheel of the wagon at left.

Biloxi's West Howard Avenue near Magnolia Street is the scene for this c. 1920 picture. It is parade day for the West End Volunteer Fire Department. The brick-paved streets are embedded with trolley car tracks. Parlor Shoe Store and Dr. R. S. Russ are just a few of the busy businesses along this downtown street.

September 19, 1940, is the date for the annual Fireman's Day Parade. Trucks from each of the volunteer fire departments were represented. Five bands, including the Biloxi High School Band, provided festive music for the parade. This truck's theme was "The City's Welfare—Safeguard America", and approximately 80 small hydrangea flowers adorned the truck. Six-year-old Sarah Tremmel, the daughter of Louis Tremmel, was the featured rider on this truck.

The priest and his accompanying acolytes and dignitaries await the arrival of the fishing boats for their annual blessings. The Blessing of the Fleet is conducted in the waterway of the Mississippi Sound. Other events coinciding with this celebration included a ball, parades, boat contests, and religious services. The Blessing of the Fleet continues to be a Biloxi tradition.

The Blessing of the Fleet is an annual celebration. The presiding Catholic priest bestows liturgical blessings upon the colorfully decorated fishing boats and shrimp trawlers. The blessings are given in two parts: the solemn liturgical blessing of the vessels and the blessing of individual boats. A wreath dropped from a U.S. Coast Guard plane was included as a memorial for the departed fishermen.

Sea Scout Ship 210 of Biloxi sailed on *Vixen* along with other ships in the vicinity. Sea Scouts are a branch of the Boy Scouts of America. During the 1940s and beyond, Sea Scouts participated in regattas and sailing races. Sea Scouting is now aimed at young adults ages 14 to 20 and is coed.

Crowds gather in front of the Saenger Theatre in anticipation of opening night on January 15, 1929. The crowd covers the entire street. Harold S. Orr managed the $200,000 theater that boasted 1,500 upholstered seats, a Wurlitzer organ, and a capacity to show Vitaphone and Movietone productions.

Mayor Jerry O'Keefe (right) and Sen. John C. Stennis (left) speak at the ceremonies for the American Bicentennial Celebration in 1976. In honor of the festivities, a time capsule was laid in the plaza across the street from Biloxi City Hall. Stennis served Mississippi well during his career, and the John C. Stennis Space Center in Hancock County is named for him as well as the USS *John C. Stennis*, a nuclear-powered Nimitz-class aircraft carrier.

Seven

BILOXIANS

Biloxians come from many different backgrounds, ethnicities, industries, and religions. The blending of cultures makes the area stronger and much more diverse. Biloxi is influenced and impacted by the military, the entertainment and tourism industries, the schools, sports, and community organizations.

The seafood industry is culturally, economically, and socially intertwined with the city of Biloxi. Emigrants from southeastern Europe during the late 1800s and early 1900s and from Vietnam in the 1970s and 1980s came to work in the seafood industry and settled permanently in Biloxi. A unique place to live and work, Biloxi is shaped by all those who have participated in its growth.

The 1930 Biloxi football team positioned themselves for the team photograph on November 11, 1930. During the 1930–1931 school year, athletics beyond team sports were introduced into the curriculum. Student athletes were expected to balance their sport with academics.

Pitcher Frank Ragland, born in Water Valley, Mississippi, visited Biloxi with the Washington Senators during 1932. They held their spring training in Biloxi from 1930 through 1935; players stayed at the Hotel Biloxi, and Biloxians came out to support them along with the City of Biloxi and the Biloxi Chamber of Commerce.

A fireman from the West End Fire Company is shown in this portrait. The uniforms were very distinct, and each fire company had a different uniform that differentiated it from the rest. Firemen would hold balls and parades each year, and the festivities were always grand.

A family stands in front of the Spanish House on Water Street in Biloxi. This area is located to the south of Jackson Street and to the west of George E. Ohr Street. The building has been used by many different groups over the years. The porches shown in this image are no longer there.

Organizers of the Mississippi Coast Historical and Genealogical Society met in the courtyard of Mary Mahoney's Restaurant. Julia Guice (left) and Dale Greenwell (second from left) pose with other members of the society in 1968. The group is still active in the community and publishes journals annually and hosts a history week at the Biloxi Community Center.

The Hass family fishing camp on Deer Island, just south of the Biloxi Peninsula, was named U.S. Camp Sonny Boy by Martin Hass and established around 1905. Deer Island was home to different groups, such as the Aken and Baker families in the early 1900s, but no one currently lives on the island.

Biloxi librarians Blondie Hartmann (left) and Florence Freidhoff (right) stand in the schoolyard of Howard I Elementary, which was just one block away from the Biloxi Library at that time. Both were influential in starting a local history and genealogy area in the Biloxi Public Library; both were also members of Biloxi's PEO Chapter E, a philanthropic educational organization.

Ruth Huls Hunt, a sophomore when this picture was taken in 1936, is dressed in her pep squad uniform and a "BHS" hat. She graduated from Biloxi High School in 1938. Later in life, Hunt became the historian for the Biloxi Public Schools. Total enrollment for Biloxi schools stood at 2,773 for the 1936–1937 school year.

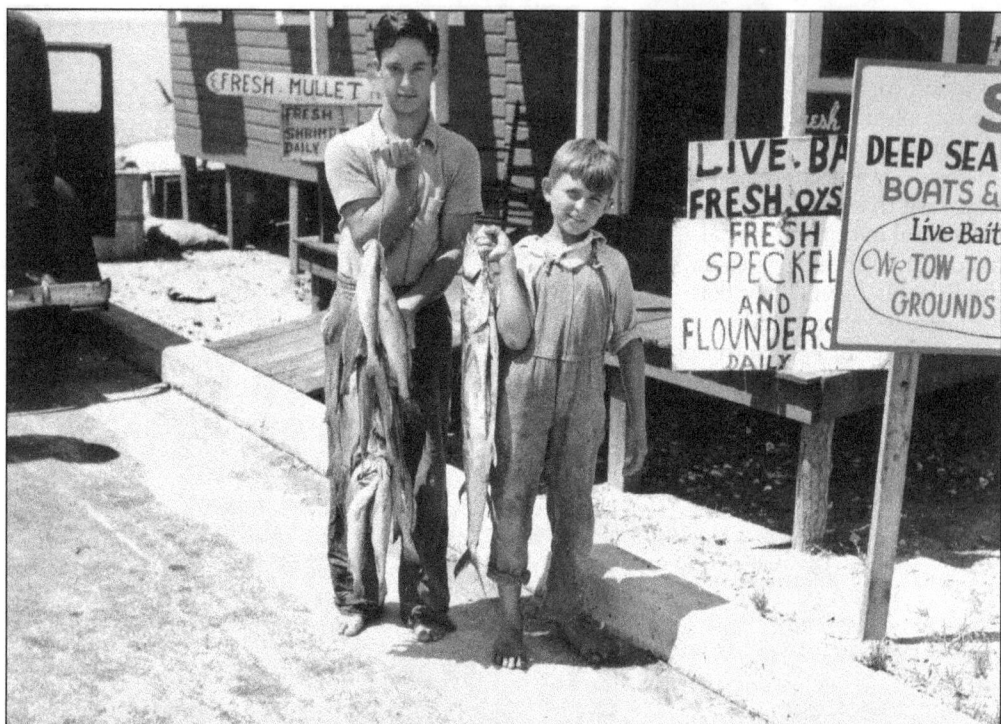

Two young men showed the fish that they most likely caught that day. They are standing near the Biloxi beach. Signs in the background show that deep-sea fishing charters are available, and live bait could be purchased at the shop. Fresh mullet, sometimes referred to as "Biloxi bacon," as well as speckled trout and flounders are also advertised.

Two generations of Biloxians display fishing nets aboard a boat. Net making and throwing are arts, and it takes skill to do both. At community programs, the Maritime and Seafood Industry Museum teaches children about net making, and employees show them how to cast nets.

Shrimp were available by the handfuls in this picture. The shrimping industry is going strong on the Mississippi Gulf Coast. If not seen on the water's horizon from the beaches, shrimp boats can currently be found on Back Bay Biloxi near the remaining seafood factories or in harbors on the front beach. Fresh shrimp can be purchased directly off the boats.

Women and men work in a factory peeling shrimp in this 1940s image. Whole families would work in the seafood industry, and all ages worked in the factories to deal with the influx of a great volume of seafood. Workers came from various backgrounds, and many people emigrated here from southeastern Europe.

A man walks beside a huge oyster shell pile near Biloxi's Back Bay. These oyster piles would collect near the various seafood factories, and this would have been a common sight throughout the 1800s and 1900s, while the seafood industry was booming in this area. Biloxi was once deemed the seafood capital of the world.

Workers on Back Bay stand with shovels in hand as trucks are ready to transport oyster shells to other destinations. Shells could be turned into grit or used in road projects. Many early Biloxi streets were paved with oyster shells, and if one looks closely, a few shells can still be found cemented by concrete in the older areas of town.

Mounds of oyster shells are piled high on the *President Roosevelt* as well as the boat to the left. These boats dock and wait for workers to unload the cargo. Once unloaded and shucked, the oyster shells could be found in piles near the various seafood canning factories.

FISHING SCENES
-at-
BILOXI. MISS.

Sport fishing near Biloxi is still a popular activity, and the catches displayed in this postcard exhibit what was available in the early 1900s. Charters are available for deep-sea fishing and also for fishing in the rivers and streams in the area.

Biloxi High School's 1923 football team sits for a team picture. At that time, the squad was known as the Yellowjackets. It was not until much later that Biloxi's team was named after the Biloxi Indians. During this period, A. L. May was the superintendent of Biloxi schools, and student enrollment was just above 2,000.

Dorothy Davis's seventh-grade class poses for a portrait in front of the Howard I School at the northwest corner of the intersection of Main and Water Streets. Harry T. Howard (1858–1930) donated the building and land for the elementary school, and it was named in his honor. Today the Biloxi Post Office, built in 1958, sits on the site of the school.

The 1907 image above shows horses pulling a fire engine and fireman down a city street. Possibly the same engine is pictured below barreling ahead as the two horses gallop east on Beach Street. The sign for the street is located on a low fence in front of the horses at right. The horses, firemen, and wagon pass pedestrians and houses on the north side of the street. Notice the distinctly uniformed fireman holding onto the rear of the wagon as it speeds down the street. The fireman's view would have been the scenic beachfront, which at that time, would have been paved with oyster shells.

Famous entertainers and personalities have always gravitated to Biloxi. The 1950s and 1960s, in particular, were years when the city sparkled with popular artists. Among those that performed during that time were Elvis Presley, Jerry Van Dyke, Dave Gardner, Johnny Rivers, Mamie Van Doren, and Jayne Mansfield. Pictured here is Jayne Mansfield as she poses on a beachfront balcony around 1967.

Pres. Harry S. Truman (right), First Lady Bess Truman (center), and A. P. Shoemaker Jr. (left), manager of the Edgewater Gulf Hotel, visit inside the Edgewater Gulf Hotel, most likely in the late 1940s. This was not the first time that Bess Truman visited Biloxi; in 1933, she brought their daughter, Margaret, to Biloxi to recover from pneumonia.

The northern end of the Maloney-Dantzler House property is the setting for this image. Members of the Maloney family are seen overlooking the chickens, ducks, cows, and horses on the property. The gazebo at right was visible from Howard Avenue. It is hard to believe an agrarian lifestyle could fit in with city life, but the animals and family seem content in this image.

A Goodyear dirigible visits the Biloxi Fairgrounds around 1919. Notice the uniforms of the soldiers surrounding the site, as they appear to be World War I soldiers' uniforms. A great crowd gathered for the event. Goodyear dirigibles, which were airships, were produced in the years following World War I.

107

Biloxians enjoy the nice weather on a sunny but most likely humid day but also seek the nearby shade of an oak tree near a harbor in the 1920s. The schooner *Julia Delacruze* is docked in the center of the ships and boats. A large movie camera appears to be on board the first boat (right).

A Biloxi girls' basketball team poses for a picture in the 1910s on New Years Day. At the time, the girls played opponents from the high school teams of Moss Point, Pascagoula, Bay St. Louis, Vancleave, and Gulfport. The basketball season at that time began in November and ended in February or March.

Louis Braun takes the oath of office on April 30, 1936, to be the mayor of Biloxi. Justice of the Peace Dewey Lawrence administered the oath, and commissioners John Swanzy and Ed Tucei stand on the stage as well. Braun served as mayor for two terms, in 1936 and in 1939.

Swimmers prepare for races from a lower pier with the anticipation of many onlookers above and below the pier complex. Rowboats were evenly spaced to track the gentlemen swimmers.

NASA astronaut Fred Haise (right) attends a ceremony at Biloxi City Hall with his daughter, Mary (left), after his return from NASA's Apollo 13 mission. At Keesler Air Force Base, crowds of people waited to greet their fellow Biloxian once again and to celebrate Fred Haise Day.

A sign on a portable billboard advertises that there would be a welcome home celebration in honor of Fred Haise, returning from his Apollo 13 mission of April 11–17, 1970. The festivities were held on May 8 and 9, 1970. The Saturday, May 9, parade started at Bellman Street and Howard Avenue and weaved around Main, Lameuse, and Water Streets.

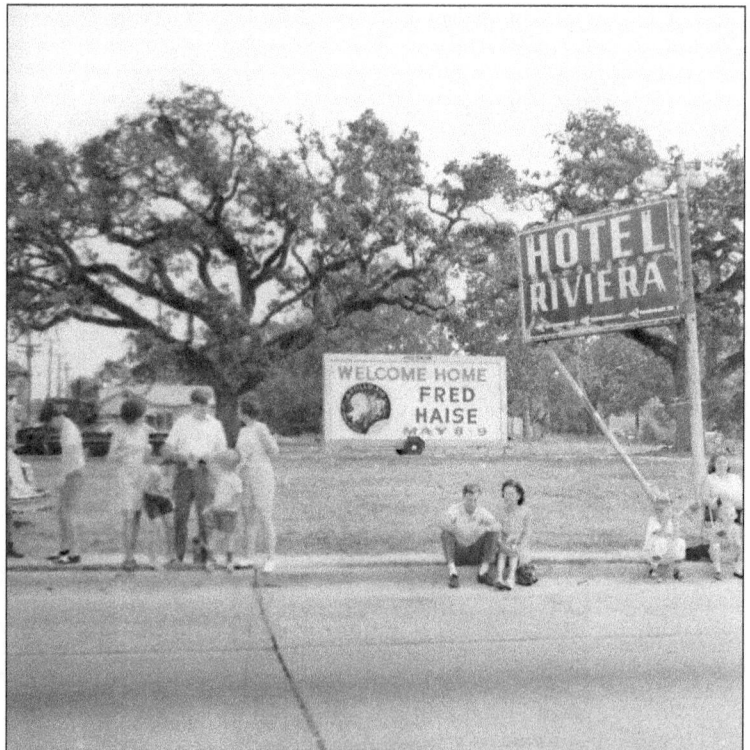

Eight

LAGNIAPPE

Lagniappe translates to a bonus, gratuity, or a small gift, and the usage of this word dates back to the 1840s and has Spanish roots. It is a popular term around southern Mississippi and Louisiana with a positive connotation that makes one anticipate receiving a little something extra.

Many of the images in this chapter are exactly what lagniappe is all about; they are a little extra of Biloxi at the journey's end. Many different scenes, some modern and some old, are contained within the following pages. Waterways, shooflies, and new views of Biloxi are a few of the places documented in this chapter.

Shipbuilding under the oaks in Biloxi was evident in the early 1900s. These two men rest briefly from building this boat under a mossy oak. Individual and professional boatbuilders have honed their skills in Biloxi, and the practice was first established to navigate the local waters and as part of the seafood industry. On the lower right, a movie camera is just in view.

Seagulls follow a luggar in the Mississippi Sound as they search for fresh food. According to the Cornell Lab of Ornithology's Bird Guide entry for the laughing gull, the bird is found on the northern Gulf of Mexico year-round, and the male and female birds build their nests together. Their call sounds like laughing, and they are known as *mouette atricille* in French and *guanaguanare* in Spanish.

A man in a kayak takes a break from rowing to pose for this scene on Biloxi's Back Bay. The calm waters of the bay are ideal for scenic views and water sports. Areas with marshy grass and islands inhabit the bay, too. Watch out for the occasion alligator as well in these areas.

An aerial view of Biloxi's bay and the 1927 concrete Biloxi-D'Iberville Bridge is shown in the 1940s. Looking north of the bridge, one can see what is now the city of D'Iberville but was then considered North Biloxi. Along the southern coastline of the bay, canning factories and schooners are actively working.

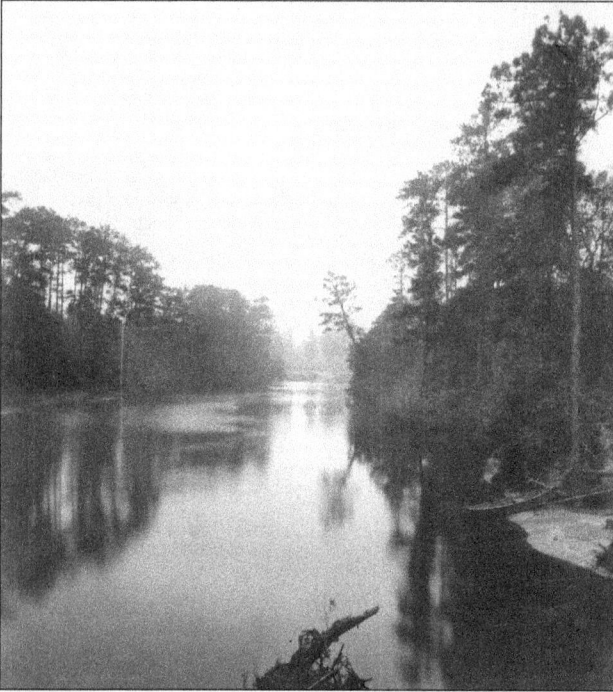

The Tchoutacabouffa River is seen in the early 1900s, and the river is pronounced somewhat like chu-ta-ca-buff. It is a great place for those who enjoy fishing and boating. Fish native to this area include crappie, black drum, speckled trout, mullet, sheepshead, and bass. Flood stage for the river is 8 feet.

Another view of the Tchoutacabouffa River with its sandy shores is seen here in the 1940s. The river is just one of many in this area, and it is an example of the natural and rural settings within close reach to Biloxians. Waterways, trees, and the influx of migrating birds, like the chipping sparrow, provide many opportunities for birdwatchers and nature enthusiasts.

Much like the architecture of a gazebo, the shoofly is a raised wooden porch with stairs built around a giant oak tree. The tree's leafy branches provide a year-round canopy that shields visitors from the intense sun. The breezy elevation provides a reprieve from pesky insects. This structure could accommodate bands, dancing, and celebrations, such as weddings. Presently, a newly constructed shoofly can be found on Biloxi's Town Green on Highway 90. A woman sits on the shoofly steps above, as two men frame either side of the structure. Two other individuals stand in the center. A shoofly had steps overarching a fence and was connected to a front lawn for easy access to the road in the 1940s image below.

Looking south from the lawn of Beauvoir, this property was a train stop on the Louisville and Nashville Railroad line and had a post office from 1878 through 1908. During that period, the property was used as a Confederate veterans home. Property owners' beachfront lots once extended to the water's edge, as was the case in this 1890s image; easements were eventually needed to complete Beach Boulevard.

The Biloxi Canning and Packing Company was located to the immediate east of the Biloxi-D'Iberville Bridge. The canning company was the oldest canning plant still in existence in 1934, and it was originally organized by William Gorenflo and Lazaro Lopez. Other local businessmen who became involved with the company included W. K. M. Dukate, Charles Redding, and C. F. Theobald, to name a few.

The stucco Biloxi Public Library is pictured in the 1970s, before the library moved to 139 Lameuse Street. The Creole Cottage (left) was located on the property until it was moved to the new library site. Just behind the library and one street east on Main Street, the northern edge of the Santa Maria Apartments is seen.

The Creole Cottage made its journey north on Lameuse Street to its new home from 1977 until 2009 in the plaza across the street from Biloxi City Hall. After the 1977 Biloxi Library was torn down, the Creole Cottage was moved to the west in early 2009 to Rue Magnolia Mall.

The Councilor Oak is to the east of the Tullis Toledano Manor House. The legend of the oak states that Native American tribes across the Mississippi Gulf Coast gathered beneath this particular oak in council. Two Native American groups from this area included the Biloxi tribe and the Pascagoula tribe.

The corner of Jackson and Delauney Streets looks very different today from the time that this image was taken in the 1960s. The back of the Avelez Hotel is seen, but it was torn down in preparation for the new Biloxi Regional Hospital. Dedicated in October 1986, Biloxi Regional Medical Center is located at the northeast corner of the intersection of Jackson and Reynoir Streets.

Rosetti's Café, located on East Howard Avenue, was owned by Vincent J. Rosetti. It was near the approach to the Biloxi–Ocean Springs Bridge between Cedar and Myrtle Streets. Signs on the building advertise po-boys, which are French bread sandwiches often stacked with fried oysters or shrimp, and Schlitz and Jax beers.

Cottage Inn Café (left) was located at 114 West Beach Boulevard in the 1940s. According to the 1941 Biloxi City Directory, it was managed by Russell Braun. Broiled Kansas City steaks, chicken, seafood, and fresh vegetables were all on the menu at the time of this picture. Gorenflo's service station (right) was located next door.

A construction crew works on Howard Avenue in the Vieux Marche Mall under the canopies installed during urban renewal. They are located near the eastern end of the mall, which ended at Lameuse Street. New building facades in some areas were also part of the construction. The People's Bank Building (left) is visible over the canopy.

The canopies for the Vieux Marche Mall in the 1970s are viewed west of the intersection of Howard Avenue and Reynoir Street. What had been a continuation of Howard Avenue was closed and turned into a pedestrian mall between Reynoir and Lameuse Streets. The canopies were eventually taken down, and now eastbound traffic is allowed to pass via the mall once again.

The Biloxi I-110 loop was in the early phase of construction in the late 1980s. The loop, completed in 1988, even had a jingle written on its behalf that was played on the local public access channel after it opened. It was named in honor of former city commissioner and Biloxi councilman J. A. "Tony" Creel (1934–1992) and Sen. John C. Stennis (1901–1995).

The Golden Nugget (right) advertised floor shows in this 1970s picture. In the same complex, another club (left) advertised an "All Girl Show" with Myrna, Cindy, Dee, and Wendy performing strip tease acts. Many of these types of clubs closed within a few years of legalized gaming's arrival. These clubs were located south of Highway 90 between Camelia Street and Rodenberg Avenue.

The Cathedral of the Nativity of the Blessed Virgin Mary is shown in 2009. Roger Morin was selected as the new bishop of the Diocese of Biloxi in March 2009. Before his selection, Archbishop Thomas Rodi served as the Archbishop of Mobile and the Bishop of Biloxi simultaneously.

Sacred Heart Elementary was behind the Cathedral of the Nativity of the Blessed Virgin Mary. It was converted into a parish hall after Hurricane Katrina. In 2007, the schools in the Diocese of Biloxi were restructured, and St. Patrick Catholic High School was built to replace Mercy Cross High School of Biloxi and St. John High School of Gulfport.

The Saenger Theatre marquee (right) stands out from the theater building on Reynoir Street; the theater was restored beginning in 1999. Looking south, the construction of the Beau Rivage Casino (right) is seen in this 1998 photograph. The Beau Rivage opened on March 16, 1999; after Hurricane Katrina, the casino reopened on August 29, 2006. The theater is owned and operated by the City of Biloxi.

The intersection of Lameuse Street and Howard Avenue is seen here in 2009. Ellzey's Hardware (right) is located in what was once the People's Bank. The Biloxi office of Dale and Associates and Dale/Morris Architects, the architects for the new Biloxi Library to be built at Bellman and Howard Avenue, is located above the store. The law firm of Page, Mannino, Peresich, and McDermott (left) is located across the Vieux Marche Mall.

Looking east from atop the Hard Rock Casino parking garage, one can view the newly renovated Highway 90 with its modernized striping, lighting, signage, and updated sidewalks and curbs. Overhead high-power lines are noticeably absent. The Biloxi Small Craft Harbor and adjacent Memorial Park are graced with ample parking. Just a few blocks away and nestled in a neighborhood of houses, the Pelican Cay condominiums tower above the tree line. The new, elevated Biloxi

Yacht Club, under construction, peeks through trees adjacent to the highway's edge. At the eastern tip of the Biloxi Peninsula, the bustling casino hotels provide the tallest structures on the city's skyline. Wide, clean beaches and fishing boats lure visitors and fishermen to the warm waters of the sound. The eastern shore of Deer Island can be spotted on the right.

BIBLIOGRAPHY

50th Anniversary Souvenir: Biographical and Historical Daily Herald, 1884–1934. Biloxi, MS: *Daily Herald,* 1934.

Biloxi City Directory. R. L. Richmond, VA: Polk and Company, 1927.

Biloxi-Gulfport *Daily Herald* 1888–2009.

Biloxi, Mississippi, Sanborn Fire Insurance Maps. Sanborn Map Company, 1893, 1914, 1925.

Dyer, Charles Lawrence. *Along the Gulf: An Entertaining Story of an Outing Among the Beautiful Resorts on the Mississippi Sound from New Orleans, La., to Mobile, Ala.* Gulfport, MS: William E. Myers, 1895; reprint Pass Christian, MS: Women of Trinity, Trinity Episcopal Church, 1971.

Guice, Julia. *The Growth of the Biloxi Public School System.* Vol 1. Biloxi, MS: City of Biloxi, 1979.

Hecht, Eugene. *After the Fire: George Ohr: An American Genius.* Lambertville, NJ: Arts and Crafts Quarterly Press, 1994.

"History of Keesler Air Force Base." www.keesler.af.mil/library/factsheets

McIntire, Carl and Bob V. Moulder. *Shrines to Tomorrow.* Vol. I. Starkville, MS: Bob Moulder, 1971.

Local History and Genealogy Department Collections, Biloxi Public Library, Harrison County Library System.

National Hurricane Center, National Oceanographic and Atmospheric Administration. www.nhc.noaa.gov.

Nuwer, Deanne S., ed. *The Buildings of Biloxi: An Architectural Survey.* 2000 Edition. Biloxi, MS: City of Biloxi, 2000.

Nuwer, Deanne S. "Gambling in Mississippi: Its Early History." *Mississippi History Now.* March 2005. mshistory.k12.ms.us/articles/80/gambling-in-mississippi-its-early-history

Skelton, Zan. *The Biloxi Public Schools, 1924–2001.* Biloxi, MS: Biloxi Public School District, 2002.

Sullivan, Charles L. and Murella Hebert Powell. *The Mississippi Gulf Coast: Portrait of a People.* Sun Valley, CA: American Historical Press, 1999.

INDEX

Visit us at
arcadiapublishing.com

··

www.ingramcontent.com/pod-product-compliance
Lightning Source LLC
Chambersburg PA
CBHW080559110426
42813CB00006B/1350